ALLEN PHOTOGR

THE CA
REPAIR OF RUGS

CONTENTS

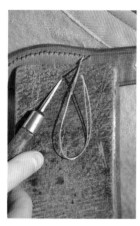

TOOLS AND MATERIALS

SEWING MACHINES

Most of the repairs covered in this book can be effected without a heavy-duty sewing machine or the need to stitch leather fittings by hand. The domestic machine shown here is fitted with an ordinary dressmaking needle and will easily manage woollen and quilted material.

RAW MATERIALS

The main items needed to repair and care for rugs are shown here. They include:
• latex glue such as Copydex
• canvas and woollen blanketing for patching and lining
• nylon web for replacing leg, breast and surcingle straps
• tongueless roko buckles for use in conjunction with web straps
• plastic fittings for use with web straps
• Velcro tape for horse boots and tail guards
• cleaning oil for leather
• lubricating oil for metal clips

TOOLS FOR HAND STITCHING

The majority of repairs in this book do not include leather and can easily be carried out with a domestic sewing machine. However, with leather fittings on day, stable and New Zealand rugs, you will need to either have the use of a heavy-duty sewing machine, or be able to restitch the fittings by hand.

To hand stitch these fittings, comparatively few specialist tools are required. They are, from left to right:

- stitching clamps • pliers • knife
- stitching awl • beeswax • needle and thread • hammer • scissors.

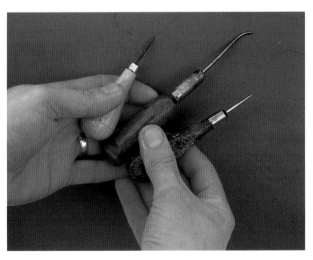

The choice of awl handles is a matter of personal preference, there is no one 'correct' type. If it is possible, try the different shapes in your hand and see which one you feel most comfortable with.

Addresses of firms who can supply such tools are given on *page 23* together with suppliers of materials and industrial sewing machines.

VELCRO FASTENINGS

This material was originally used by astronauts in space capsules and has been adapted to suit a variety of uses. With horse clothing, it is mainly used on boots, bandages and tail guards as it offers firm and positive holding power, coupled with the convenience of quick removal.

Velcro does, however, have an awkward habit of picking up and holding fluff which can impair its performance. Even washing will not remove it and picking it off by hand is often the only answer.

Light, domestic-weight Velcro should be backed onto material or web for strength, although the heavier weight type shown here is strong enough to be used double thickness.

HORSE COMFORT

When bandaging, make sure that you tie the knots where they will not cause any pressure points on a horse's leg. This can easily be avoided by using bandages which utilize Velcro instead of tape ties.

NYLON WEBBING

Nylon webbing has gained immensely in popularity over recent years as a cheaper alternative to leather, especially for stable headcollars and rug fittings. It is very strong, but is susceptible to fraying and being eaten through by rusting metal fittings.

It is, on the other hand, easy to maintain because any fraying parts can be immediately sealed over a flame. The heat momentarily melts the nylon, and the repair process can be improved by tapping the molten web with a hammer.

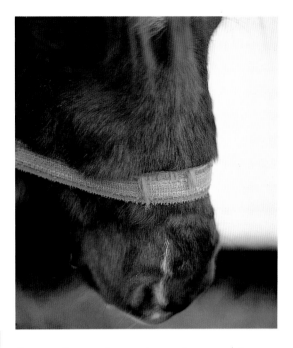

HORSE COMFORT

Always check that the ends of the web do not have any sharp edges which could rub against the horse. This is particularly important if you have just sealed the nylon webbing in a flame.

Any ordinary domestic sewing machine should be capable of stitching through nylon web but check the condition of your needle before and after working on it as nylon is notorious for taking the edge off needles.

HAND STITCHING LEATHER FITTINGS

BASIC TECHNIQUE

Single-needle stitching is all that is required to replace leather fittings on rugs. The pictures show the various stages of hand stitching which is common to the several types of repairs covered in this book.

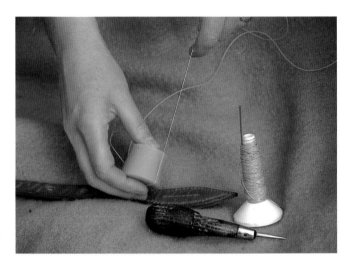

Having cut a length of linen thread, pull it through a piece of beeswax. This will help to protect it from the elements of the weather, animal sweat and abrasion in addition to preventing the thread from fraying while you stitch with it. The next step is to thread a blunt-ended needle onto one end and tie a knot in the other end.

As you will be stitching towards yourself, position the work in the clamps with the end of the stitching farthest away from you. Once the work is in the clamps, hold them between your legs while sitting on a chair. By firmly squeezing your legs together, you will tighten the hold of the clamps on the work being stitched.

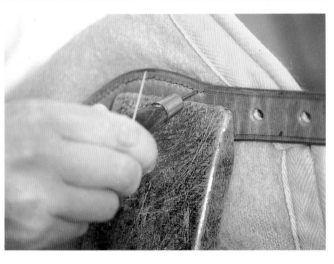

Having secured the materials to be stitched correctly in the clamps, commence stitching by first inserting the awl through the second to last stitch mark on the leather.

With the needle and thread, follow the awl blade from the left-hand side, through the work to the right-hand side. For the first stitch, pull the thread through until the knot holds against the back of the material.

Return the needle to the left-hand side by passing it through the end stitch mark, so forming the first stitch. Continue to stitch towards yourself, first by inserting the awl one stitch mark back from the last stitch, then bringing the needle from the left- to the right-hand side of the work and returning it to the left side through the end of the previous stitch. After the first stitch you always lift the large stitch at the back when returning the needle there. This helps to keep the stitches even and flat.

Once you have completed the length of stitching, finish off by tying a single knot as close to the back of the work as possible and cut the remaining piece of thread off next to the knot.

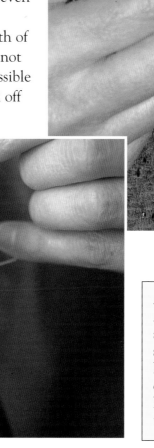

Author's Special Note
All the instructions and pictures for hand stitching are for right-handed stitchers. Those of you who are left-handed should reverse the instructions.

RESTITCHING LOOPS

To restitch a loop, insert the end of the loop between the leather that forms the buckle piece as you put the awl in for the first time. Take great care that the loop is only inserted to half the width of the leather to which it is being stitched.

Continue stitching to where the other end of the loop will fit in but, before inserting the second end of the loop, make the two or three holes that will be used to stitch the loop into position. It will be necessary to stitch half of the loop from one side and the second half from the other side so that the loop may be moved slightly to one side allowing the awl to be used in a straight direction rather than at an angle. Be extremely careful not to try to lever the loop into position with the stitching awl or the awl's blade will snap. Make sure that the loop is large enough and move it into position with your fingers.

With single-needle stitching, the stitch on the right-hand side of the work – the top surface when the rug is in use, A – will always be half the size of that on the left-hand side, or the underneath, of the work, B. It is this larger underneath stitch which helps to give strength to the piece of work by gripping more of the weave of the material, while the top stitch which lies on the top of the leather, is smaller and neater.

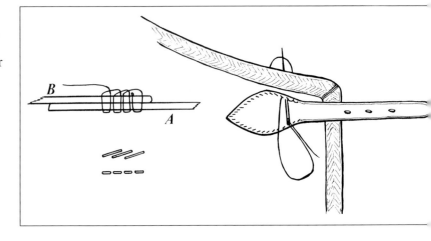

NEW ZEALAND RUGS

REPAIRING TEARS TO THE CANVAS

Tears like this are best treated by gluing the outer canvas to the woollen rugging inside. Use a wide-faced hammer and force the glue into the weave of the material. A domestic sewing machine should be able to cope with two thicknesses of canvas and one of rugging, as long as you do not machine over anything thicker such as the back seam.

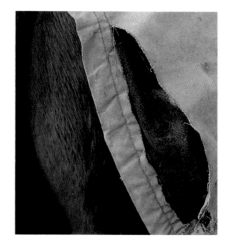

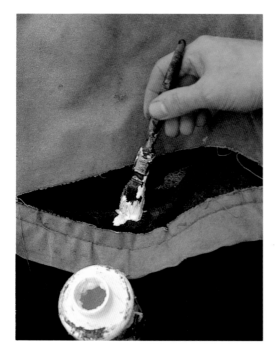

Barbed wire can be lethal, especially with turn-out rugs. (*see above*) This small tear can easily get caught on the wire and become a major repair job. It is possible to patch the tear while the rug is still on the horse by feeding glue under the canvas and using a piece of material underneath as a patch.

A more permanent repair is possible by covering the tear with a patch and machining round it. The picture shows the rug on a heavy-duty Singer 45K sewing machine, but it is perfectly feasible to stitch the patch on by hand. As explained before, use a hammer to aid the penetration of the glue into the material.

HORSE COMFORT

Many types of rugs can be improved and made more comfortable for the horse by adding a piece of sheepskin-type material along the wither part of the neck. This can first be glued into place and then stitched to form a permanent feature.

(see picture at foot of page)

REPAIRING LEG STRAPS

The clips used to fasten New Zealand rug leg straps are prone to collecting mud and thus failing to operate properly. Keep them moving freely with a regular application of oil.

If the leg straps of your rug are leather and need replacing, consider using nylon webbing in its place. This is easier to work with, is cheaper and makes equally good leg straps.

Replacement clips can be easily stitched onto web either by using a domestic sewing machine, or else by hand stitching. If hand stitching, the size of the stitches can be gauged using the weave of the web.

The leather fittings on many New Zealand rugs are advertised as weather-proof but in my experience they will still benefit from a regular coating of leather oil.

HORSE COMFORT

The correct way to fasten leg straps is for each strap to fasten up at the back of the rug on its own side, crossing around them-selves in between the horse's legs. This helps keep the straps off the inside of the horse's legs and friction is kept to a minimum. (*See picture on the right*)

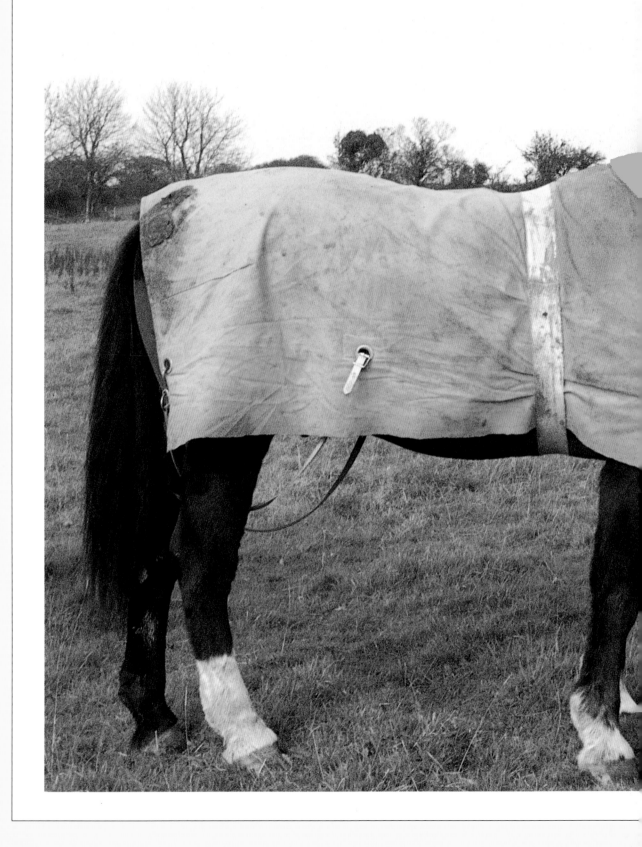

HOW TO PROLONG THE LIFE OF A NEW ZEALAND RUG

The working life of a New Zealand rug can be greatly extended by regularly carrying out this straightforward check list.

• Always keep a supply of small patches and glue readily to hand for instant repairs.Minor tears quickly become major undertakings.

• Keep clips well oiled and free moving.

• Regularly oil any leather fittings even if they are advertised as weatherproof.

• Ensure that the leg straps and surcingles are the correct length.

• Seal any webbing fittings at the first signs of fraying.

• Try to restitch any fittings before they come adrift, either by machine or hand.

• Re-proof with a wax dressing to maintain the rug's weatherproof qualities.

• After a season's use, thoroughly clean and store the rug in a dry location preferably where moths will not have access to it. Metal rug chests are ideal.

RE-PROOFING A NEW ZEALAND RUG

Even the best quality canvas New Zealand rug will loose some of its weatherproof characteristics over the years.

To re-proof the entire rug, first apply a coating of wax cotton dressing. This is exactly the same as the dressing used to re-proof wax coats. Then heat the surface of the waxed rug with an ordinary hair dryer. When warm, the wax will melt and be absorbed into the weave of the canvas.

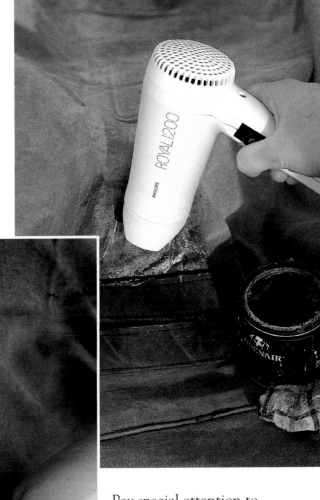

Pay special attention to the central seam and, if the rug has a surcingle or cross straps attached to it, the areas where they are stitched onto the canvas.

Smaller areas, especially the central seams, can also be proofed using a propriety seam sealer. This is squeezed out of the tube and rubbed into the canvas by hand.

STABLE AND DAY RUGS

CARE OF RUGS

Many repairs to stable and travelling rugs can be avoided by regularly checking the inside of loose boxes and horseboxes for any protrusions such as bolts that could snag a rug if a horse were to lean or rub against it. This is especially so of the string anti-sweat rugs.

I have lost almost as many rugs during storage as on the horse. I have now learnt that by putting a bar of strong-scented soap in the rug chest, moths are kept firmly at bay, but this does not alleviate the necessity to wash all rugs, numnahs and horse boots before storing.

RUG FITTINGS: LEATHER

If your day rug has web fittings, then you will have no problem washing them. If it has leather fittings, however, you should consider removing them before attempting to wash the rug. Although leather, if well oiled, can take a certain amount of water, once it has been through a warm machine wash with soap or detergent it is never quite the same again. So, unless you intend to carefully hand wash the rug and keep the leather as dry as possible, decide whether or not to remove the buckle and point first. When the rug is washed, they can be restitched onto the rug as described earlier in this book. All this may sound somewhat long-winded, but a good quality woollen day rug is well worth the extra bit of time and effort.

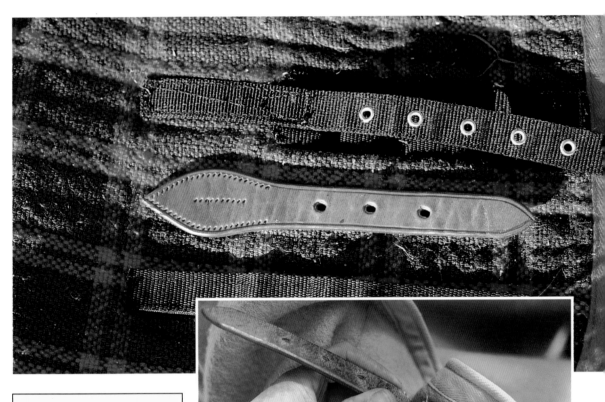

HORSE COMFORT

Whenever you have finished stitching a fitting to a rug, always use a hammer to tap down the underside of the stitching. This will ensure that there is nothing standing proud which could rub the horse.

RUG FITTINGS: WEB

If the breast straps on your rugs are leather and require renewing, then they could always be replaced using webbing and a tongueless buckle. There are several types of tongueless buckles on the market, the two most popular being:

The roko buckle This is a metal buckle which is very strong, but it can rust if left damp. It should always be remembered that it has a top and a base to it and care must be taken to fit it correctly as in the picture; the wider bar and the movable round wire loop must be at the top when the buckle is done up.

The plastic, lay-flat buckles *(see below)* The two parts of these plastic buckles are each attached to webbing and lock together to fasten. They are relatively strong and are completely washable.

ANTI-SWEAT RUGS

'A stitch in time…' as the saying goes, but there are far more than nine stitches needed in this example. Mesh rugs never last forever if used constantly. However their useful life can be greatly extended by regular washing and, as mentioned, checking the horsebox for any rough edges.

The only practical way to repair a mesh rug is by painstakingly stitching each broken piece of material by hand. If you have caught it in time and there is only a couple of links broken, this is a practical proposition.

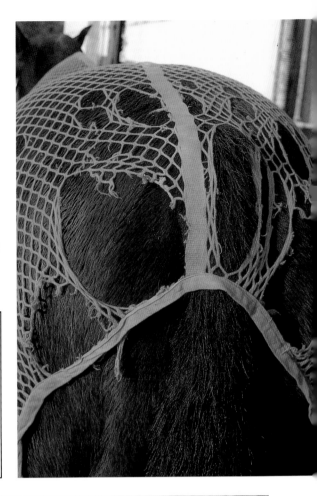

HORSE COMFORT

When buying an anti-sweat rug, always select one which is a size smaller than the horse or pony's usual rug size. This will help prevent it from extending over the horse's rump causing him discomfort, and will also reduce the risk of the horse 'sitting' on the rug and tearing it while travelling.

ROLLERS AND SURCINGLES

Great attention should be paid to preserving all leatherwork, not only on rugs, but also on such items as rollers and surcingles. A regular coating with saddle soap will keep them pliable and help to prolong their life.

Any material that cannot easily be washed should always be dried out after use. This includes the padding of rollers and the felt used in protective clothing for travelling.

HORSE COMFORT

If you need to shorten a roller or surcingle, always take a tuck in the web and stitch the three thicknesses together. Never shorten it by tying a knot in the web. This will only cause a pressure point on the horse or pony when in use.

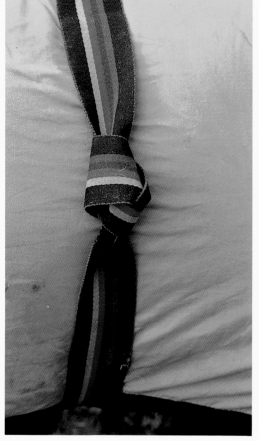

NUMNAHS

Regular washing of numnahs is essential to remove an animal's salty sweat. A numnah, however well washed, will often wear at the point where the girth of the saddle lies.

There is only one way to avoid this and that is by stitching or gluing a piece of leather or other hard-wearing material along this part. Suede, such as that used in riding chaps is ideal as it is often washable. Most soft skins could be used although washing can then become a problem. Heavy-weight cord works well and can be stitched either by machine or hand.

HORSE COMFORT

By pulling the numnah *(see left)* up into the arch of the saddle, you will not only extend its life, but you will also make it more comfortable for the horse as there will be no chance of any pressure being put upon his withers.

PROTECTIVE TRAVELLING CLOTHING

TAIL GUARDS

Protective tail guards can be made from a material to match the rug, or else from a hard-wearing fabric or leather. With all leather tail guards, oil the body and the strapping regularly. Should the leather straps need renewing, they can be replaced using web ties as a substitute. Velcro can also be used as a means of keeping the tail guard closed.

TRAVELLING BOOTS

Most travelling boots use Velcro as a means of holding them in position and should be regularly inspected for any wear. Regular washing and brushing with a stiff dandy brush will keep them in a good serviceable condition. *(see below right)*

HEAD GUARDS

There are several patterns for head guards and most consist of felt with a leather covering. Keep the leather well oiled and always dry the felt after use.

HORSE COMFORT

This improved design of tail guard offers an extremely high degree of protection and comfort for an animal's tail. By cupping underneath the tail and then extending high above the tail's base, there is no gap left for a horse to 'sit' and rub on while travelling.

PERSONALIZING YOUR RUGS

Day rugs and summer sheets can easily be personalized by adding the owner's initials, stud name or logo.

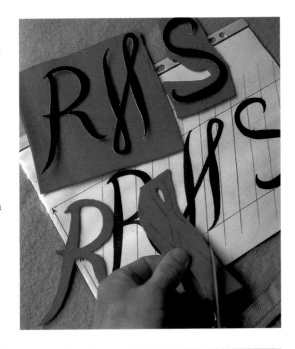

To make an initial or logo, first design, mark and cut it out of a piece of light-weight card. Transfer this pattern to the material and carefully cut it out. It is important that the edges of the material chosen will not fray when cut. The next step is to either tack stitch or glue them in place on the rug and leave to dry, this will help when machining. Finally, machine around the initials to make a permanent feature on your rug.

An alternative is to put the pony's or horse's name on the rug.

SUPPLIERS OF TOOLS AND MATERIALS

Apart from the stitching awl and clamps, none of the tools and materials in this book should be hard to find.

Fastenings, glue, clips etc. Hardwear and camping shops.
Material Patches for rugs can be taken from defunct rugs, old jeans, dressmaking material and tent manufacturer's offcuts.
Needles These are sold as blunt-ended darning needles in needlework shops.
Thread Plaiting thread is ideal for hand stitching. It is also sold as carpet thread.
Beeswax This is often available from honey farms, health and chemist shops and it is also sold in candle form.

SUPPLIERS OF REPAIR MATERIALS AND SPECIALIST TOOLS

Craftwares Ltd., Home Farm, Hotham, York, YO4 3UN.
TEL. 01430 423636.
J.T. Batchelor Ltd., 9–10 Culford Mews, London, N1 4DZ.
TEL. 0171 254 2961/8521.
Le Prevo Leather, Blackfriars, Stowell Street, Newcastle upon Tyne, NE1 4XD. TEL. 0191 261 7648.

SPECIALIST SUPPLIER OF CANVAS, RUGGING MATERIAL, WEB AND FITTINGS

Tambour Supplies, 4A Penbeagle Industrial Estate, St Ives, Cornwall, TR26 5ND. TEL. 01736 793305.

SEWING MACHINES

As already mentioned, an ordinary domestic machine will, with a sharp needle, tackle most of the jobs in this book. If you should like to acquire an industrial machine, then the following firms will offer helpful advice.
J. & B. Sewing Machines Co. Ltd., 3 Coverack Road, Newport, Gwent. TEL. 01633 266495.
Sew Rite Sewing Machines, 45 Ropewalk Road, Llanelli, Dyfed.
TEL. 01554 759833.

British Library Cataloguing-in-Publication Data.
A catalogue record for this book is available from the
British Library

ISBN 0.85131.659.X

Published in Great Britain in 1996 by
J. A. Allen & Company Limited,
1 Lower Grosvenor Place, Buckingham Palace Road,
London, SW1W OEL

Illustrations by Robert H. Steinke
Design and Typesetting by Paul Saunders
Printed in Hong Kong by Midas Printing Ltd.